Honorary Astronaut

MARY AUSTIN SPEAKER —

Here are these orbiting poems
for you, my new

Honorary Astronaut

but remember :
it's lonely out
in space !

Blast off —
— Nate

Poetry

Nate Pritts

GHOST ROAD PRESS

Library of Congress Cataloging-in-Publication Data.
Honorary Astronaut
Ghost Road Press
ISBN (Trade pbk.)
13 digit 978-0-9816525-1-1
10 digit 0-9816525-1-4
Library of Congress Control Number: 2008932292

Cover Design: Scott O'Connor for GO Studios
Layout and design: Sonya Unrein

Ghost Road Press
Denver, Colorado

ghostroadpress.com

ACKNOWLEDGMENTS

Thank you:

Anti-: Morning Ice.

Conduit: Collected Poems.

Court Green: New Year's Eve.

DIAGRAM: Sad Girl-I-Did-Not-Stop-To-Inquire-Of.

Elsewhere: My Backyard.

Forklift, Ohio: Blue-Feathered Life, Early Morning Television, Hi There, Today I Am & Various Kinds of Fire.

horse less review: Circus.

M Review: After four or five times.

Mustachioed: Talk-Talk

Pacific Review: Sunrise, Sunset.

Pilot: Big Expectations & Tin Rhino.

POOL: Blue Car.

Salt Grass: One for Carol Ross.

Softblow: Scarecrow & This one red leaf.

The Southern Review: Brown Tree, Yellow Bird & The Prime Mover.

Stirring: A Priest of Zeus.

The Bedazzler, an online feature of WAVE BOOKS, first published "Joyous Effusion, Ending Perplexedly," "I Am Full of Missing," "This Tremendousness I Can't Talk About," "A Day Sort of Exactly Like Today" as "My Mix-Up," "Delegate Flower" & "Mortality Effusion." Thanks to all the good people there.

"The Trouble I'm In" was written for, & first published in, the Cy Gist Press anthology *My Spaceship.*

"Action Poem" was included in *Open Windows III* (Ghost Road Press, 2008).

"Brown Tree, Yellow Bird" was included, along with an essay describing my revision process, in *Poem, Revised: 54 Poems, Revisions, Discussions* (Marion Street Press, 2008).

"Collected Poems" is inspired by the Kenneth Koch poem with the same title.

"I Am Full of Missing" is for Matt Hart who gave me the title.

"I Believe" is archived at the website for National Public Radio's series *This I Believe.*

"Lake Effect" was included in *The Bedside Companion to the No Tell Motel* (No Tell Books, 2006)

"New Year's Eve" was reprinted at Verse Daily on 3/13/2007.

"One for Carol Ross" previously appeared in my online chapbook, *The Happy Seasons* (Swannigan & Wright, 2004: www.thematter.net).

"Today I Am" was written in response to two paintings made by Danny Hagan & was produced as a limited edition broadside to commemorate the 2nd Annual Civil Rights Conference held at Northwestern State University, in conjunction with the American Democracy Project.

Thanks to Matt Dube & Matt Hart & Clay Matthews & Scott O'Connor & David Saffo & to Mission Control—Kate, Dylan, Laney; Oscar, Maggie, Andy, Wally

& above all: Rhonda.

Contents

The Prime Mover 15

There's a Leaf for That 17

Sad Girl-I-Did-Not-Stop-To-Inquire-Of 18

Lines 19

Today I Am 20

Brown Tree, Yellow Bird 21

I Am Full of Missing 22

Various Kinds of Fire 23

One for Carol Ross 24

Hi There 25

Afternoon Stars 26

This Tremendousness I Can't Talk About 27

Complaints about the Green Room 29

Blue Car 30

Joyous Effusion, Ending Perplexedly 31

The Road to X 32

Scarecrow 33

This one red leaf 34

Morning Ice 35

You Can't Put a Price on This 36

Tin Rhino 37

Love Everything 39

Circus 40

Sunrise, Sunset 41

Red Couch 42

Cog 43

Action Poem 44

Collected Poems 46

My Backyard 49

A Priest of Zeus 51

All Those Stars 52

Effusion after Walking Oscar   53

A Day Sort of Exactly Like Today   54

Delegate Flower   55

Mortality Effusion   56

Why Should I Say I See the ThingsI See Not?   57

I Believe   58

Electronics Shop   59

Big Expectations   60

Not Tuesday   61

After four or five times   63

Talk-Talk   65

October Monday Light   66

Blue-Feathered Life   67

Lake Effect   69

Instrument of Surrender   70

The Trouble I'm In   71

New Year's Eve   72

The Prime Mover

Surely even the accidental under-the-table tap
of one foot on another, heel nuzzled close to arch,
can signal love! Surely even our smallest actions

have celestial significance! Deep in the cosmic brain,
stars flare into life while others snuff out.
What kind of a world do we live in when a piece of music

played the right way can send us swimming out
into deep water? It's so easy for us to get lost,
directionless & soggy & far from shore.

For some journeys there is no map & all that matters
is the beautiful scenery. But who can really say
if the empty stretches of grass that stretch emptily for miles

are more beautiful than the billboards screaming
all my wants as I drive past. Many attempts have been made
to define beauty, to find some universal formula for it,

& then the head researcher dies, his notes lost. Or else
they're not truly lost; they're just illegible, cramped & shaky
between skinny blue lines, the equations unbalanced.

Termination is a constant theme. Encounters with beauty
can lead to forgetting your umbrella in a strange restaurant,
to overfeeding the parking meter. *How much time does one need*?

is a question worth considering when, later, the silence
of no change jangles in your pocket. The restless foot
seeks assurance that it's not alone but you must be careful

when interpreting the signs. A coat left lonely on the subway
may mean cold times ahead in only the most literal sense.
It may take years to find a replacement, the sleeves & shoulders

a perfect fit. Long blue stretches may await you, coatless
mornings when you hurry to finish your coffee
before that last swallow goes cold. So many unfortunate souls

held their mugs too long & went thirsty, unwilling
to compromise. They would look up to the bright stars & wonder
why they were chosen for this persecution, why they

were the ones being tested. But the light they sang to
was old light. It had to travel for years to be seen.

There's a Leaf for That

Today I'm pretending that each leaf
has a hidden inner life, I'm pretending

there are too many different kinds of joy
& curling sorrow, of thin-veined rage,

of yellow & orange happinesses, for me to ever hope
to catalog or fathom. So: the car that cuts me off,

there's a leaf for that. Again & again I fumble
with the cosmic thread, the small eyed

universal needle. Always fail; always
missed mark. There's a leaf for that.

Confronted with undones, left to deal with lack.
There's a leaf for the whole range,

the unpredictable human pendulum swing.
There's a leaf for that, I say, pretending, looking dead on

at something cracked & crumbling in my hands.

Sad Girl-I-Did-Not-Stop-To-Inquire-Of

Don't ask me who she was, crying
her blue blue eyes out on that hollow front porch
I walked right on by. Me: unblinking, hunched;

her: sobbing, boo-hoo. It was almost 6 pm,
fall, the early darkness & cold. Her sorrows remain
unknown; don't ask me why she cried.

I'll never know what she might have felt but,
in my head & heart, she feels it forever—
long nights of autumn sadness, pine needles

bunched in smug fists up & down the branches
hanging over her porch. I had my own problems
but no one caught me pulling my hair out

on Main Street, yelling with rage in the parking lot.
At least I had the good sense to keep myself
to myself. I had my own problems then, & now too.

I have my own problems now! My own colossal anger
& a sadness like overgrown grass but I miss her
& would comfort her & would build a house

for us to move into together, with no front porch,
no loneliness, & one great big front window with curtains
we could open or close whenever we wanted.

Lines

Let's say for example we were damaged last week,
last month or last year. The pain or loss occurred in the past.
That's great! Today is today! No pain today is good.

But let's say we were overjoyed

last week, last month or last year. Then that happiness
occurred in the past. No! No! I want to be happy today
& keep all my happy yesterdays right here & now too!

But isn't the memory of happiness also a kind of happiness?

Isn't the memory of pain even a kind of happiness since it is a memory
& memory is the only way we can prove to ourselves
we exist & have existed & have a chance at continuing to exist?

I think I must be one confused sad/happy animal to feel this way.

Bright colors & balloons make me happy, so just imagine
how a bunch of brightly colored balloons would make me feel!
Imagine each one popped & then what?

The sky is so much less blue than it was. But is it less blue

than it would have been if it had never been filled with balloons
of any kind? Should I make it my life's goal to fill the sky
with balloons again, in a strictly literal way?

What if you bite into an apple? Should you never bite into an apple

simply because you can't always & forever be biting into an apple?
Certainly not! Apples are delicious whether or not they continue
into the cavernous future of your mouth's experience.

Today I Am

It is today & today I am
1 2 3 spiders on a string, I am ten animals

all at once & I am
screaming at you to let me be the one

animal you pick out as your own. I am
talking about my emotions, no matter what

it sounds like I'm saying, I am
talking about my soft head, my soft heart,

my love. Outlandish color combinations
have no effect on this hollow feeling of

something that splits me ragged. If only
I had the words. The words are morning

yellow, sun bright cold, & endless
dizzying black & hopeful white &

razzmatazz orange &, O, gigantic red!
O grammatical pause, O stupefying

break. O big something inside me: I am
a spider through & through, hazy, luminous

self held by a string &, yes, I am
the string that holds me & the outside

thing the string holds to. I am
sleeping & in my sleep my dreams are of me,

the screaming one, unsure. I am
the thing I lost & I am the one looking for it.

Brown Tree, Yellow Bird

If only everybody knew where the sweetest bliss was to be found!
Imagine the raucous dogpile that would ensue, making it impossible

to get a table near the window without a long wait
or reservations made months in advance. I have reservations

about everything. Luckily, most things are out of our hands because, O,
the many zany & pointless things we'd do to ourselves if we could.

Bananas in the bowl on the kitchen counter turn slowly brown
& nothing I do will stop that. I'm helpless in the face of many things:

flat tire, spoiling fruit, the color yellow. The idea of wood, so solid,
terrifies me. My big hands grasp & grasp. The house I left

because I thought it was sapping my strength has a big brown tree,
leafless in November, with one small yellow bird, nesting.

During certain times of the year, the ratio of bird to tree is higher
but these are the days of proud sole ownership. I list my many failings

with examples as I drive my car through the stop sign
at the beginning of my neighborhood, the stop sign that never works.

I've thought seriously about changing my name
to make it more complicated & ambiguous, harder to pronounce;

long into the inky night, I've wondered about dyeing my hair yellow
& learning to live with what I can't live with. My fears can save me

is something I wrote on a leaf, then stuck to the bottom of my shoe
so I could walk it off. Tuesdays I pretend I'm that lonely yellow bird,

scared that I might fly away & scared that the opposite might happen,
that I might stay & sing beautifully.

I Am Full of Missing

A school bus screeches to a stop
signaling to its passengers that the heady demands of knowledge
are subject to the same laws of velocity as the stunning

leaf hitting the stunned ground or the clouds
that run smack into each other. Meaning
there are certain things we can't move past

without at least stopping to say hello.
Even then, who knows if we'll find some way to get by?
Observers say the bus stopped

because the street was clogged with jaywalking turtles.
Such a cavalier attitude
on the part of the turtles, to walk, or on the part of the observers,
to open their eyes & look at just anything. Life

is like that, we are tempted to say. You're zipping along
& exactly what you didn't think was happening
turned out to be what was really happening. Everyone else

already knows & behind the wheel there's a driver who cares
too much to just barrel over whatever is in the way.
We are tempted to say that talking seriously
about the state of the world

demonstrates our seriousness about the state of the world.
We are tempted to say *Form follows function* or *The trend
this fall is bright colored tops & layering & then crumbling.*

Just ask the leaf. Surrounding each of us is a vast cushion
of something missing & we're all
honorary astronauts sent into the vacuum to report back.

We are tempted to talk in the third person
to generate a kind of distance from the mothership
as we rocket towards discovery.

Various Kinds of Fire

Two times the shattering racket of the phone
ringing & each time my fish are startled
right out of themselves, gliding silent behind the glass,

disappointed, like I am, with the late night wrong numbers.
Count yourself lucky, Jack, that someone is trying
to reach her sweet midnight voice out to wherever you are

to ask you over or say she's sorry, one thousand thousand times
sorry, & she wants you back. Two times the phone rings
& then I have to put up with the phone not

ringing through the rest of the long & hollow night.
Mathematicians can't prove that one is the loneliest number
& their order's great sorrow is that the gods

they pray to can't even tell us what
we already know. They'd like to sing a song
that could wake up the whole town on Christmas morning

& get us all to look under our prickly green trees
with the soft eyes of love & hope. Who knows
what amazing trinkets we'd find if only someone told us

where to look? Under my sink, dusty but proud,
a stoic fire extinguisher & already I'm starting to feel
safer. Scientists say there are various kinds of fire

but when they burn they all burn the same, a crisis
of individuality so deep & desperate that I'm stunned
speechless. In my world, we would all get our own personal flames,

color coded to match with our shoes or skin tone or
our bestest intentions, & Christmas would be everyday,
there'd be presents everyday & when the phone rang

it would always, always, be for you.

One for Carol Ross

When she says "I haven't made my bed, except to change
the sheets, in three & a half years,"
Carol Ross is trying to say all there is to know about Carol Ross
without saying any of it: disheveled beds
breed disheveled minds or vice

versa. But what bearing does one's physical condition
have on one's mental state? What connection can we assume?
For three long days I drove through Texas, stopping only to sleep
& eat &, for three long days, I was followed by the police,
those diabolical minions of the law; they switched cars often

to make me doubt. They would have liked nothing better
than to see me fold like cheap bed clothes laundered
one time too many. Every morning they'd be there, parked
up the street, waiting to begin the chase. But
do we really want to catch that which we chase?

Or vice versa? I'd watch the shadows of my hands shake
on the wrinkled hotel comforter. Each of those three long days
I wore a sweater a pretty girl had slept in; I could still smell
her in the chunky wool cords & it calmed me.
When I finally crossed into New Mexico the sweater came off;

on the third day I changed into a shirt that smelled good
in a sweater-a-pretty-girl-slept-in kind of way. I was confused.
Maybe the scent I thought was hers was mine all along.
I felt cheated. I was unable to make my bed for years after that;
Texas still scares me. What I'm getting at
is simple, something about (a)

the author's inability to love himself or others or
(b) the nature of paranoia, which is to say the question is not
"Am I paranoid?" but "Am I paranoid enough?"
or (c) such beautiful laziness when faced with a tangle of sheets.
How long can it really take to straighten things out?

Hi There

I am a tiny leaf that is lost to its branch
& is wind-tossed & sad & lost
or I am like a lost leaf because a leaf

is such thin sorrow & you, you know this
because you are also a leaf or at least
like a leaf in your demeanor; see how subtly

your hands move, giant seagulls swifting over
whatever oceans rage with joy below us, or rather
your hands are like giant seagulls, rounded & white,

swooping over something like an ocean
that rages, overjoyed at their own ridiculous love.
"Hi there" is the casual greeting I've selected

for use today & will use again tomorrow
if the correct amount of money is applied to the account
before the balance dwindles to nothing.

I am like an overdrawn account in that
you cannot acquire anything of worth by using me
& you know this

because your ledger is often unbalanced if by ledger
we can agree that I mean mental/emotional state
& certainly we can agree can't we? We can agree

on so much it makes our disagreements shrink
like birds dotting the horizon or like clouds
swept away by high winds which is one more thing

we can agree on, that the clouds are clouds
or are at least exactly like clouds. They are things
you can't touch & hang out of reach.

Afternoon Stars

Rainwater splashes through the gutters, persistent,
while baby hornets no bigger than a pinprick
ram themselves into the wall again & again with a too-audible

thump! They want out, badly, is the Morse code translation:
we all want out. Then these three women walk in
like a car crash replay, like the minute before

you're allowed to leave the place you don't want to be, these blondes
simply amazed at themselves & a man near me puts down his sandwich.
He can't hold it anymore! Suddenly, what he needs is too heavy.

Certain well-chosen stimuli, once introduced, can permanently
change an environment without even so much as a *pleased-to-meet-you*.
The sky is starless; the single branch in my heart

is weighed down by all this starlessness, but my head knows better,
knows that the stars never really go away, blinded-out
by the too-bright sunshine on afternoons similar to this one.

On afternoons similar to this one, it dawns on me
that I am the item in the series that doesn't belong—my hat has one stripe
instead of two or my jacket has one button too many.

I am almost overcome by an urge to spill the beans, to sing
like a bird, to scream "It's my shoes that set me apart!"
In a controlled experiment, you can predict what might happen.

At night, you can expect those sun-hidden stars to poke their shining faces
through the coarse black blanket of night. You can assume
a fruitful connection between items in a closed system.

All night & all day, those women are running rampant
through my head & I'd voluntarily crash my car into every single falling
raindrop if it meant I would get home faster.

This Tremendousness I Can't Talk About

Just about the only thing I can say,
if you need me to say something,
is that there is right now this tremendous
unspeakable tremendousness pulsating
around me like one thousand stars
about to flare & shoot out at one time,

or maybe even more than one thousand stars:
one hundred thousand stars! A big number of stars!

Or, more precisely, this tremendousness
is like absolutely nothing else,
because it is its own thing. I realize now
that my earlier metaphor, of the stars,
isn't quite right because it sounds sensational or
spectacular or cosmically significant...

which it is, I suppose, this tremendousness,
this unutterable & inexplicable tremendousness

that fairly quivers both inside & outside my very me.
So here I am sitting in my car—my green car—
a correspondent, baffled, unsure
how to say what I am compelled to say.
Me scratching my head, me perplexed,
me so tremendously overwhelmed

that everything I am seeing right now all goes
bye-bye every second & is replaced

by something so equally tremendous
that I want to tell you all about it, too,
but am afraid that there are no words I could use

that would get it right. Meanwhile
certain signals from the outside world
indicate that I need to move ahead—

a green light from a metal box, or from the trees—
though I really don't want to.

Complaints about the Green Room

I live my whole life inside, walking
as carefully as possible to lessen my chances of a fall.

I feel I am living in a big plant, my office deep
in the hollow stalk, levers & gears to control the slow

unfurling of petals, a button simply marked "Grow."
There are days when the green room holds me

& the way it holds me makes me remember
my mother. There are days when, I can tell,

the green room would just as soon let me go.
My fear is that the green room might one day forcibly

expel me from its green peace. My fear is that I
might one day massacre the green room, tearing

at its rough walls. If I have a complaint,
it is that the green room cannot exist in me

the way I am forced to exist in it. Light tumbles
from my windows, pale broccoli-green shade changing

to rich spinach. My thoughts remain blue, a wave.

Blue Car

That blue car you drive just passed by
but without you in it, without anyone in it, actually,
which raises more questions than it answers.
Perhaps it wasn't moving at all & I was!

It was me, zipping around town in my own car.
Other things that are or could be blue:
a canoe, the sky, a comedian's act, fingernails
on a Saturday night to complement a killer dress.

Here I would like to offer a brief but incisive comment
on the transitory nature of the vehicles we attempt
to navigate through the raging woods of sadness:
for years I piloted a green car & it became a part of me

but it is long gone & I am still me but not.
These days I drive a white car, mostly, though
some days I find myself behind the wheel
of a shiny grey car &, as there is no explanation

for this, I won't even try to fake one. Now
that I think about it, I remember that you yourself
drive a fancy brown car these days, when you drive at all.
So when you didn't whiz by me in your blue car,

it wasn't even you that didn't pass me without waving
or stopping & urging me to get in, to forget about whatever
this life has turned in to & start driving the old cars
the old way forever, forever, oh my, forever.

Joyous Effusion, Ending Perplexedly

I am here, now, & that fact
calls to mind such unbelievable fields

of blunt white snow, by which I mean
joy-at-possibility,

suddenly I am like a whale swimming in a whole ocean
of himself! Like a cloud with some sky

floating in it. Now I am here
but I know that someday soon I will be

remembering my here, my now,
& that will be unbelievable too,

like seeing myself in a mirror
when I'm not even standing in front of one!

Now joy, then joy, joy building itself
a complex architecture to reside in,

radiating until I have no idea
what it is that can make me happy.

The Road to X

Remember plan B, the old switcheroo,
the map to X swapped for blank paper

& then the rug pulled out from under,
the bum rush, the delicate escape. O sweet filet,
O tender piano teeth: now comes the pursuit, now

the pitter-patter, patter-pitter & the soft strains
of love. Bold or unbold, I'm on the way

& when I arrive the townspeople would be smart
to bolt their doors quick, to flip their *Open, C'mon In!*
signs to *Closed*. Come back soon. Dinner

or late night snack or unendurable & vast emptiness
of the soul, I'm hungry for something

& according to the map, buried just underground:
treasure. Between two trees, another tree;
between two stars, open space, a vast separation.

I've been following this path my whole life,
railway towns & bus stops & cold every day.

Now, all of a sudden, I'm the country's darling?
I'm not the man anyone thought I was—weak eyes
& shifty chin hidden beneath a fake burly beard,

broad swaths of flannel & quiet rage.
I did not ever chop down a tree

that didn't deserve it in the worst way.
I'm working on an alternate route, mach 4, version 7.0,
moving from plan W to plan X but I've forgotten

my shovel. I have no way of getting deep enough
to enter the dream I've been dreaming.

Scarecrow

As the party winds down we take turns
clubbing the dolphin piñata—

with plastic sword, with silver broom handle—

exactly the same way some she
once slammed her channel-changing heart

into mine, dopey & complacent,

but instead of candy what spilled out
was eight months of slow-time,

instead of confetti making the real world bright

there was a crumbling erosion of the self,
one thousand thousand tiny pieces.

For weeks, scatter. I'd like to look at a leaf & not

remember, to feel a spring breeze & have the option
of a soul temporarily dead to all that implies.

In a vast room where twenty slim doors lead into

twenty rooms, you can bet I'll open the right one last
leaving a series of startled occupants & interrupted

musical notes in my wake. The green bug is not my ache,

the eruption of weedflowers not my untended
emotional capacities.

Straw man—the leaves inside you are dead leaves.

This one red leaf

that I pinched off the waist-high bush branch
as I walked the sidewalk path

at exactly the same moment as my eyes fell
on the empty green iron bench

made me think of the profound lonely screams
of empty benches everywhere

& everywhen, causing me, bursting, to reach out
to grab whatever was in reach,

this one red leaf absolutely the softest leaf,
of any color or season,

ever to be plucked from the branch, ever to be held
between two clumsy fingers,

scrutinized & caressed, called *memory*, rolled up
& called *blessing*.

Morning Ice

I'm driving straight into each & every snowflake
that dares to get in my way to prove something
final & crushing about the inevitability of my actions, the gospel

of trajectory that states it doesn't matter
how you get where you're going. Thousands of screaming
fans roar their approval! Their hunger is voracious;

their eyes devour. They love the resultant slush.
They are fans of aftermath but share with me a healthy fear
of long division. They prefer quick goodbyes, the kiss off.

No one wants to think they could lose everything they have
just like that. I am blinded by the stiletto light of sun
on these snowy days. Even though I am driving, my car

is like a couch shaped like my car & not moving.
The audience, those who are left, react with shock
& disgust. I've said nothing but implied so much

by the evocative positioning of my eyebrows learned
through long hours staring into the bathroom mirror.
There is a weakness in me so strong everyone can tell

I'd rather sit down than stand up. I'd like to punch you out
for what you said is the kind of thing I might say to someone,
though it is well known that I have trouble making a fist.

I am blizzard-driven; I am a snow-covered pier. I wish
I could melt myself away & whisper my wet secrets
to the asphalt all through the asphalt-black night

while the sun sleeps & the moon glows & I harden over
like glass. In the morning,
put one careless foot on me & find yourself falling fast.

You Can't Put a Price on This

When you walk in, your name
will be on a card that lets you know where to sit.

You will be surrounded by smiles & this shouldn't
unnerve you; there will be kids cheering
the wonderful new designs you've shown them.

Your melting poker face. Wet streets in New York &,

thanks to the miracles of the modern age,
it is 1974 & you are there. The world was sometimes
black & white, sometimes color & how vivid

the colors, how stark the lack. Two losers
drink coffee together, discussing, comparing notes.

The pieces are hidden in plain sight,

magnified, says one of the losers, but out of reach.
Did you mean to knock over the pencils?

Was that a part of the act? Remember, despite
the broadly smiling faces, there are people here
who think you're an embarrassment.

Focus groups have indicated your inner uselessness,

also that blue shirts make you look more confident.
Face to face, we can accomplish so much.
We can figure out how much I am worth to you.

We can set a fair price for what I'm offering
once we determine what it is.

Tin Rhino

Duty-bound, outdated relic, forgotten:
the tin rhino stands outside—forever
outside—bolted to its rough wooden podium. Tin rhino: refugee
from some dream, well-intentioned but inarticulate
statement about the rogue mechanisms of nature,
rampaging animalistic machinery.

Thousands of grass blades, crushed under the tin
rhino's tin feet, scream silent green screams.

★

Jokes (overheard) at the expense of the tin rhino—

: I wouldn't sit near that end
                                        (*points*)
      of the tin rhino!

: Can it hear me? It can't hear me.

: (*of birds nesting in his open metal mouth*)
                                        they don't know what
            they're getting into.

: I wonder who made it,
                        that old sad rusted beast.

★

Knock & echoes where his heart should be.
It waits for us to pour ourselves into it. Out of place,
clunky, ultimately useless, the very existence of the tin rhino—
of any tin rhino—forces us to recognize our own tin rhinos.
He (*it is a he*) asks us (*he begs us*) to tell him what
to do with his comical horn. Should he tear
open the sky, can he hope to catch the passing clouds?

*

Love song of the tin rhino—

Please: acknowledge my wanting.
Please: I notice you.
Please: stand close.

Let me steal three smiles & look at your body alive.

Love Everything

All that happens is that I am made
to feel small when I think about
the vast spread of these patio umbrellas,
how they work equally well

at blocking sun or rain & how
I don't work well, no I don't,
& you would not say LAUDABLE!
& shake my hand, firm in your white shirt,

your smile, & you would not whisper
FUNCTIONALITY HIGH to any others
in reference to me no matter how generous
you were feeling so I say O—

I am a poor busted abacus, you can't count on me
& I say O—in response to your query
I can't say how I'm doing, the results
are not yet in & somewhere strawberries

pop out like knuckles from a closed fist
& somewhere a smile flashes by me,
not too inspiring—reassuring maybe but nothing
to change your life over &, yes, I can hear

someone humming a tune. Rain or shine
there is a place for the useless,
all of us lined up with leaves covering
our eyes. We so love our vacancy

& the sun is too bright & we can't
help but love, love something, love
everything & nothing because that
is what we're good at.

Circus

In my new myth of the whole world
& how it all works or doesn't,
the delicate yellow fish girl loves
blue water boy & would further love
to plant many a fishy kiss upon his sea foamy cheek.

All of this on a turtle's back.

A rain crashing down all night
that turned out to be tears.

Then, the giant green bubble that bounces
around the sky & sounds like all voices together,

like the tv & traffic & noise & noise,

distracts both of them & leaves them together
separate, staring, & then a flash
of green light & the giant green bubble expels
the pale gray man who looks lost & homeless
&, yes, helpless. For about fifteen days.

The yellow fish girl feels compassion
& the blue water boys feels drenched
to his blue-water soul with fellow-feeling.

The pale gray man, expelled from the giant green bubble,
decides he can't live like this & wants
to get back into the giant green bubble
& so makes a song about it
that he'll sing whenever he is most lonely.

All this happening while our friends are perched
on the tip of a wolf's tongue. Waiting.

Sunrise, Sunset

Too many birds chirp in the tree
outside your bedroom window or else

it's just one loud squawker doing different voices.
Nothing but rain for the last three days

& the TV says four more until the clouds
break. You can't expect it'll clear up over night;

some things you need to wait out, you say to yourself
as the hours clunk by. Suddenly, orange.

Sunrise, sunset. Suddenly it's a week later
& you're missing even the storms

you've lived through. Some things remain
unchanged. That lonely bird still talks to himself

through the night & if you wanted you could end it
once & for all. Hack limbs from the tree he calls home

until the stripped trunk fools the bird into thinking
it's winter, that he should fly off somewhere warm

& find something else to sing about.

Red Couch

We don't usually call the stars by their names
but there was that one time we looked up
into the open darkness & said "Hello Cygnus-1,
your light is the most stunning light
reaching me tonight from so many thousand years away."
When the woman no one knew snapped my picture
she said "Be careful!" & "Systems can be dynamic

or static but either way they degenerate!"
Her eyes were shining with the same intensity
as Cygnus-1 on a clear April night, or else
it was the lingering effect of the camera's flash.
At home, I leave the lights on all night to avoid feelings
of loneliness because there could be nothing
out there in the dark & that's horrifying!

After a long day, I bury my nose in the fake orchids
on the table & say "Hey baby" for practice
or I sit on the red couch with my feet on the table.
That the couch is more burgundy than red, more
cushioned device for reverie facilitation than couch,
makes no difference. I invite my friend Cygnus-1 over
& we argue about the relationship of past actions

to present state & he says things like "People still
look at me for my bright youth when these days
I'm red as a couch." Quickly, I ask someone
to take a picture but when the film comes back I'm left
with more questions than answers: can we be more
than who we are? I look at my smiling self in the photo,
glassy-eyed & waiting to be judged.

Cog

I'm heat, pure heat, walking around in a haze
of me, the red orange purple uncertainty

that comes with the not quite night, the ending
but as yet unexamined day. The opening

of vast & previously shut doors is always followed
by the closing of same. But without a doubt I can say

I like the feel of your tired foot atop my tired knee,
O gently snoring muse. Here's sad sorry me unable

to write my goodbyes: so long, Ruffled Feathers.
hasta la vista, Disgruntled Wishes. My spirit

attaches to a balloon so I can watch it rise.
Who is this, talking about wanting all the same things

as me, stealing my jokes? The voice on the tape
sounds nothing like my own. Just now I dreamt

I was dreaming of wearing a blue coat
while wearing my old blue coat. Don't you see?

Instantly, I was satisfied. I knew I had won!
I wanted to wake your foot & every other part of you

to say, yes, I am the complex mechanical part
in your fully automated future, baby!

Action Poem

Forgive me but I'm already imagining
fifteen different calamities
as I look at your eyebrow's delicate arch
& study the vague curves of your ears.
These words I'm saying with this device
I call a mouth are generated by random
& complex processes. It's impossible to know
if they're right. Today is summer

but high winds indicate it's best to stay indoors.
What I mean is, I've got my eyes
wide open as I take one step forward
into this raving & irate future I gladly embrace.
The green light is green

only because I say so & I'm confident
my perceptions are mine. This is a power
I've reserved for these middle days of the week
when I begin to doubt the dual concepts
of blast-off & splashdown, when I often feel
the need to create my own world
to try & live comfortably in.
The more I stare at that empty space,

the more convinced I am that it is
only empty, not vacated or waiting,
& that I don't have to fill it.
Mailbox hinges creak & suddenly
I see years of people who've sent no word.
What the tree says about this is nothing
good, I'm afraid. A large leaf tumbles

& rolls across my windshield then plunges
down just exactly as it did years ago
to someone else & even one thousand leaves

can't tell me the answer
that gets me out of the mess I'm in.
That's what art is for: I could paint two squares
on a canvas & call it a person; I could
point to this splatter & call it a life.

Collected Poems

RUSTED CEILING SUPPORTS

The disastrous blue of my cool Tuesday home.

POINTING & LAUGHING

Flux, flex, flummoxed: I'm capricious, I'm dog-tired.

I'D LOVE TO LOVE YOUR APPLE PIES

Dark green interior & the seething—O my Mathematician!

WHY ARE YOU IN MY KITCHEN?

Ever present wordlessness, a shrug, this blank: _____ .

RECYLCING THE SUN

There's a bursting in the bursting of my bursting bursting.

I HATE THAT PARTICULAR SHADE OF YELLOW

All these horses in my head reduce me to trampled.

I THINK I STOLE MY NEIGHBOR'S CAT

Purple warning: late dinner.

ALLEGATIONS

Out of business, my dusty old sugar-feelings.

THE WEATHERMAN'S FORECAST

Such rackety racket. Clunkety clunk.

ORANGE SYMBOLIZES WHO I AM

Julie is my favorite month.

LAST WALK AROUND THE PARK

Silly hawk!

MURDER

In the backyard is a backyard.

WHY MY KUNG FU SCHOOL IS
CLOSED FOR THE SUMMER

Who can tally the numerous ions? The numinous son? I?

BROWN PAPER BAG

At night the crickets sing blue hollow huzzahs.

SCREAMING FIRE IN AN EMPTY ROOM

The loneliness of football fields, my empty green expanse.

TOO MANY POCKETS

This proliferation: teeth gleaming white!

WIDE RULED PAPER

Leaf-rot hullabaloo.

I COULD NOT SEE EVEN WITH MY GLASSES ON

For the love of monkey.

BIG GREEN BAG

Who knows what evil lurks in the hearts of men?

A CLOUDY DAY

Lunch time & still the birds quarrel.

THE LAST TITLE I COULD THINK OF

O wondrous car keys, my lovely tarantula!

My Backyard

My daytime backyard pretends
there are no twinkly stars overhead,
that there is no nighttime & that green
is the color of forever.

My interstate backyard is a busy thoroughfare,
the late last dream of mass transit, a sleeping bus.

My Kafka backyard thinks it is a bug.

My anarchist backyard blows up the freighter
because it believes the finality of docking
is a tyranny we should overthrow.

My second Monday of March backyard
has chilled green feet & can see its own breath
as it exhales grey worries.

My backyard of infinite sorrow wears an armband
to indicate its quiet rage at some loss.

My backyard of grape soda is bubbly
& colorful & rots my teeth when I hold it in my mouth.

My backyard & its many voices hold a press conference
which is attended by backyards from all over
each longing to hear the one sweet sound that makes it all right.

My sleepy backyard has one dream
every night for weeks
(which to a backyard is an eternity).

My backyard with one foot out the door
writes me a note to say where it is going,
illegible scrawl with tight loops
& starkly leaning characters indicating only anger.

My blushing backyard gets embarrassed easily.

My laundry basket backyard is big enough
to hold all my clothes.

My backyard in the front yard
has days when it wishes no one knew
its secret name or the secret handshake
necessary to gain access to the clubhouse.

My bestest backyard ever deserves a party
but is so busy it can never attend.

A Priest of Zeus

A priest of Zeus has a tough job.
For instance, he might have to say things like:
The omens were good that day you brought us joy—
be the same man today!
Where I'm from, that kind of talk
can get you a punch in the mouth
faster than a Delphic oracle could yell "Duck!"

A priest of Zeus has to handle being called "Priest"
all the time, never by his first name,
which is a slow & persistent sorrow. Think about
your own name grown rusty with lack of use!
Also, no one ever invites a priest of Zeus anywhere.
Friday comes & the long Theban weekend
stretches out empty as the Acropolis

twenty minutes after a play ends.
People think, "Oh, it must be great to be a priest of Zeus,
for doesn't the Big Guy constantly call you up
& give you all the inside dirt on our wretched state:
which town He'll flood or who He'll transmogrify
into a wolf-demon for real or imagined slights,"
or people say, "If I were a priest of Zeus

I'd tell Him to turn you into a cloud & let the sun burn you off
for letting your dumb sheep break my fence again."
What people don't realize is that it's not a two way street.
Zeus never asks His priests for advice
about who to rape next, or which city-state to favor
in whichever dispute.
Zeus never has the priests over on a Sunday afternoon

to drink ambrosia & watch the game on his Olympus-sized tv.
A priest of Zeus lives a sad lonely doomed human life.
He's reminded of it by his boss every day.

All Those Stars

This deep-red mystery, my color-coded flaw, I'm so sun
blind I forget to be grumpy this fine fine day, forget too
that the error in my programming is that each finite moment

passes me by to land in a big messy pile in the somewhere
back there instead of stringing together in a sequence
to be proud of. Last night I wished on the first star I saw

& what I wished for was that more stars
would show themselves & when that suddenly happened
I felt as rich as a rich king in someone else's story.

There are so many valuable lessons to be learned
from stories. In one, the beleaguered soul
wakes up ten minutes too late to catch the #6 going uptown—

it could be hours before another uptown connection
comes through!—& this is a story about how we never catch up
to ourselves or a warning that all those strategies

we employ to wake ourselves up don't always work.
All those stars that popped up after I wished them into existence?
You'd better believe I wished on them too. Soon

they faded, & so sad the fading. Running headlong,
we wish for a wall to hit, believing that this big crisis
of forward motion follows a principle of physics

that will be enforced & that someday we'll stop dead
in our tracks, signaling we've arrived
where we set out to go & that this scar will heal.

Effusion after Walking Oscar

Dog tired, we two let night's chill
air wrap us: him splayed out flat
like a six-fingered hand, me

in my blue chair & nothing else
separates us. Earlier, Oscar was
sniffing through the fields, bright pollen

from the tall grasses & weeds
dotting his nose & then there's my face
always stained with the search.

Leaves against the night sky
are just leaves, but against the night sky.
Listen: I remember our recent walk

as if it were ten years ago. Then
the answers, at least, were negotiable.
The same moon would have been shining

as it is, as it was, as it will be & that moon's
loitering is like a leash in my hand,
holding back something that would run

to the only light in a dark field & stay.

A Day Sort of Exactly Like Today

Cherries after a rain shower, apples
after days of sun bleaching. O

what a washed out &/or relatively clean world
we find ourselves welcomed into

today, August twenty-sixth! The trees
fold their leaves in defiance, grass

grows slowly. In my mind, I've been waiting
in a long line to get on this one ride

& though it looks scary it can't possibly be.
Birds & clouds fly all the time!

Are they terrified of the sky? No!
My mind always tumbles backwards.

Does that mean it's afraid? There is so much
fun to be had on a day sort of exactly like today

when we can all see that what we want
is just a few bodies ahead of us,

that it is shining & beckoning
& that it is ostensibly safe.

Delegate Flower

It is past my bedtime & I do not care
to discuss it with you, or that the only heroic thing about me
is a long time gone and even though the lemons

in the bowl on the counter shine in the static
light of the only-this-day-new moon, dammit,
I'm still writing with the same pencil

that I pulled from the washer where it must have been
in the pocket of some unwashed something. Clunk-clunk
went the pencil in the washer but now it says O!

I can no longer remember what seemed worth all the yelling
or why everything I say is covered in thick fur
or some kind of slippery plastic coating or some kind of,

well, what I mean is that, whatever it is, it's not exactly not
right but certainly isn't exactly exact. I mean
the words I'm saying should be I'm heartbroke

& I'm a sorry emissary from a sad-lonely place that is so far off
I can't even return to it. What I mean is that I'm convinced
flowers bloom all over the yard but it's so dark

& I'm so lazy that I can't offer any proof. Instead
I offer the whale blue tear, cried from my own eye.
It is full of something jaw-droppingly important to me,

if not to you too. Pretend that it is a flower
& that some better version of me picked it for you.
This flower will report its findings to the real flowers

& they will decide whether or not to grant your secret wish.

Mortality Effusion

I am not afraid to die. I am afraid to die
before I tell you what I'm thinking & what I'm thinking
is that everything decays & crumbles & falls

into pieces & even big big statues in the desert
look whole under the sun one day then
their visage is shattered the next.
We all get played

like harps in the window. I can't imagine
the pain I would feel if my burnt foot
kept me from walking with friends. Pain

in my heart & soul as well as my foot.
Still there is the wind, the wind
that acts like I used to act, like I want
to act again. So I say I am a leaf.

I say let's look at something stunning
together or not together but let's look
at the same stunning thing & realize

that if we die dead right now
& nothing we've done lasts, or even if it does,
we have this one moment, the two of us
with our souls on this bridge with a river under it.

Why Should I Say I See the Things I See Not?

I can only count up the ceiling tiles so
many times before I start to lose faith
in the ability of our senses to ascertain
any inkling of the divine. We move in so slowly,
open-handed, only to watch through tears

as the great big Blue Butterfly of Truth
stumbles away from our clumsy grasp.
Everything shifts, like my car
when I tell it to go fast & then
to slow down. It gets confused

about what I want which means it's like me,
except for the interchangeable parts.
It can replace what's broken; all those gears & cogs
hum a tune called something like
"Getting There," or "Holding Soft Hands

We Make a Better World." Up above,
the Blue Butterfly of Truth links wings
with the humongous Orange Butterfly of Unerring
Directional Sense & the enormous Red Butterfly
of Early Rising while my theme song

"10 Seconds Too Late (I Wish I Wasn't Always)"
begins & those wings
beat perfect time as I wait for the chorus—
the only part I know!—singing *what would you do
if you got in on time & how would you know it anyway*?

I Believe

I believe in the ability of puny-old-Me
to overcome most obstacles. I believe the fist

I make with my right hand in the clear blue afternoon
signals something true & lasting

about my inner state, & that an open palm
held out indicates depth of character

or at least unfathomable wanting.
I believe there is a light which, when lit,

illuminates the darkness but which, I admit,
might not conquer all. I have a flying horse,

& I believe that this assertion, blurted out
at just the right time, could make the party

fun & unpredictable again. I believe the cool temperatures
we experience at night come not

from an absence of heat but rather the presence
of something unknowable &, yes, I believe

any of us can know the unknowable without changing
its essentially unknowable nature.

I believe that deep in the swamp
there is a frog humming.

Electronics Shop

Five hundred rebel balloons crowd the open
sky, each one its own particular
color of hope & in the classical painting version of this

there is somewhere in the lonely background
an empty hand, & that would be the artist's
statement about Loss. What tremendous loss,

all this present absence of things not heretofore
absent. Stubbornly we knock around, all the livelong day,
collecting stuff to later lose. From behind the closed door

at the end of the long hallway in my head,
a tinny voice talks about how once the red wire
plugs into the blue-shaded slot that poor slot

will weep many thousands of blue-shaded tears
if the red wire ever even thinks about delivering its energy
to any other slots. Giant schematic diagrams

unrolled on the floor show absolutely no reason
why this should be so. But we know it is. So
all the music in the world is sad & no matter what

you order, the restaurant messes it up. Badly.
The real loss is that we're, none of us, very good
at being machines but still we try, we try. The real loss

is all those balloons, giddy with freedom, will get no farther
than the ragged winter trees with their ragged ragged hands.
Colorful new leaves dominate the horizon but last only so long.

Big Expectations

It was a movie about people
surrounded by trees & trapped
by the bark or it was a heavily researched report

about the qualities of charismatic leaders
or it was a song, you know the one,
that goes *na-na-na-na, yeah yeah.*

This was on the Sunday after
I didn't see you all weekend
& you were eating breakfast in Memphis

or else it was that Thursday
we ate Chinese around a crowded round table
when we really wanted burgers

or it was that Monday holiday
when we didn't want to move.
I know the sun was yellow in a blue sky

although maybe it was raining & had been
for weeks & would keep pouring.
Somewhere, a bird. Someone we didn't expect

to be rocking in a chair on a porch
was, in fact, rocking in a chair on a porch
& our big expectations were shattered

& shattered, every day shattered.

Not Tuesday

The early gray sky promised
a rainy day & under that assumption
I allowed the wind to run screaming for joy
through your morning hair.

I could already imagine droplets of water
dotting the hood of my car!
Meanwhile, Sun had other plans
& was setting in motion a complex

plot to burn off the clouds
resulting in the reemergence of yellow
& blue. Today, thought Sun,
is Sun-day! How many birds

were startled & shaken & had to spend hours
adjusting the tone of their songs!
All those plants had to open up again
& send coded messages to their roots:

no water today...just hang on....
I had to rethink everything I had thought.
Everything I thought would be a good idea
was no longer appropriate.

Calendars everywhere blushed
because it was so obvious how wrong
they were. Later, on the television news,
the man talked about the disaster so slowly

even his teeth looked forlorn. His forehead
wrinkled amazingly so we could tell
it pained him to admit what had happened.
"Something happened nobody could have expected,"

he said. He said, "Don't ever get your hopes up."
I looked at you & my eyes
concocted elaborate gestures of consolation.
Your hair still looked mussed & now

there was no good reason for it.

After four or five times

I start to get wise to your dirty tricks, silly World.

My hand again & again on the stovetop burner,
inflated & cartoon red, throbbing epically, & then

my hand not on the burner, an absence of the necessary
heat & two ingredients go uncombined,

no slow bubble & no boil over. In the pot,
equal portions of my inexplicable needs, my inability
drive. Driving, I take the long way home

& claim a scenic interest in this town, O World,
but who really wants to ride past the hollowed-out

architecture of inadequacy, the should-have-known
better? When I get wise, my head blows up big
& a mountain springs up solely for me to sit on top of

so I can dispense advice, dispense four quarters for a dollar,
dispense with the pleasantries so as to get more quickly

down to business. Which is this, grand & floating World:
you can fool me once & yes you can fool me twice

& probably even three or four times but then watch out.

I'm trusting, but not stupid. Darkness closes in
around the trees on my mountain like a simile,
all aesthetic value derived from comparison.

Substitute one term for the other & evaluate.
My legend grows like my shadow from noon until sunset,
which is scheduled for 8:13 tonight, but you know that,

you Cosmic Spinner you. My shadow will soon disappear
& there'll be no record of how I did on this test.
Grade me on a curve, O World, you sweet benevolent globe,

you dirty rotten scoundrel. Award extra points
because I tried, because I finished in the time allotted.
Give partial credit for the work I've shown

even though my answers never seem to be right.

Talk-Talk

It's time to sink or swim, put up or shut up,
but here's that early morning light again

to work its way into my brain, that mess
of tangles I keep sheltered in my head,

& my legs are bending now because I'm a man
sitting on a bench & sore uncertain

if the resolute will is what's called for,
wondering too if the clouds are the ones

that have it figured out, white sheen
tending gray even today, in this, with me.

Beyond the shadow, a shadow.
Just in the nick of time, I realize the ache

I've been feeling is a lingering shot in the arm
that shot itself out, the world set afire

then quietly quelled. Believe it or not, I disbelieve
a lot. I don't think you're even listening

though I write you poem after poem, O you
whoever you are. When I travel, I move

off the beaten path; I flap past clouds.
I am my own soul, buoyant, & all this talk-talk

can't stop me from knowing I'll float or drop.

October Monday Light

If I say the light of this Monday morning is a light
unlike any other it is because of the quality & arrangement
of the light atoms as well as its inherent Mondayness,
its Octoberousness. This October Monday light

is too soon transmogrified from now-light to then-light
though thankfully new light takes its place. Gosh!
Right now I'm undecided if this is all
a mind numbingly horrendous thing or cause

for an ecstatic & jubilant new dance I will invent
complete with corresponding vocal. I write the poem
& then I don't write the poem & the things I wrote
when I was writing as well as the things I didn't write

when I was thinking about what to write—all these things
only happened once! Who can live like that,
always watching the ocean liner of your life cast off,
bon voyage, every minute but also

how could you live holding onto each crumbly leaf
in your big clumsy hand? I write the poem & then
I don't write the poem. I get distracted by the clouds
which are there & then not & then there again.

Blue-Feathered Life

Even cluttered with branches, the sky
lets one bird slip through & even

looking at my favorite tree bud with spring

can't stop me feeling I'm sixteen, like it's night
& I'm throwing pebbles at a window no face appears in

to tell me hello, to unlatch the screen & let me in.

The flashing lightbulb sign across the street tells me the temperature
& it's gone up three degrees in seven minutes, a rate of increase

I can't figure out. Even so, my teeth chatter; I'm turning blue

as I remember my old hapless insights & still
I can't bring myself to talk about anything

but myself. You wouldn't know it but I'm sick

of poor-me & broken-down-me & even quietly-dignified-me.
Scientists say there are various kinds of fire

but, except for their colors, they're all the same.

Sunlight falls through my tree's new buds in patterns, chopped
& cut full of shadow, a jigsaw that makes me remember a poem

I never wrote about my hope for a graph to explain the soul

& that one smug bird chirps & warbles overhead, his beak full
of twig. I'm jealous, uncertain of what to say & to whom.

I've seen cars roll through the corner stop sign

five times already, recorded the changing direction of the wind
by studying the movements of the rooftop flag when suddenly

the temperature drops three degrees in two minutes. Surprisingly,

nothing changes. Is this a noticeable shift? Is it even worth
mentioning? I've imagined following that bird home to watch him build

his nest, to listen in when he talks to himself about himself, shameless,

narrating the happy story of his blue-feathered life, squawking his head off
at every morning's unexpected sunrise, convinced

it was the first, the last, that it was happening just for him.

Lake Effect

It is the time of the sweater, oh yes,
stripes & polka dots, solid colors too,
& it is the day of the jacket, newly purchased
or rescued from the deep hell of closets

to live again. I wish there were more to say.

I wish I could shape the diaphanous
steam of my breath into fabulous new words
that would cause the prettiest girls to freely give their smiles.
Elements of the landscape can hide the subject

worth viewing. As evidence, I cite this phone pole

behind which I completely lose you. The key
to my soul's dormant joy is your right big toe
painted bright red. Imagination
allows the whole foot, the leg. Forgive me

my clueless wanderings, my urge, my go, my lack.

Forgive me my rage, my range, my vehicle,
my tenor, my sax. Forgive my prayer for more
sweater weather, for a long forever
of snow & wool.

Instrument of Surrender

We imagine the red light blinks not

for us, that there is some haphazard conspiracy
of the dog-tired self. The clock tick-tocks

its maddening loss-narrative & you

don't stop. The ten rules I thought would help me reach
lunchtime unscathed by this slowly crowding world

are not, as of now, working. For whom the blinking

red light? If not for us? Immediately
I'm calling for backup, whelmed over with lack

but this is already the end I'm staring at.

At last, the center comes to me & I am far flung!
Four petals fall from the winter-white rose.

I've had enough of this. I've had enough of this.

Grey sky, peril, bird-left are my feelings
when I stare out with my newly empty eyes

upon the now vacant fields of play,

my eyes once full of sunlight, the knowledge
of distance. If only there was a song about it.

If only someone had reached this point & kept going

to show me that it was possible. Unutterable,
the phrase meant to end it all. Silent, I sign my name.

The Trouble I'm In

With everyone else around me
in cryogenic hiber-sleep,
I'm the one who has to land this bird,

this big spaceship with its busted combustabator
& interstellar pixatrix drive. Or maybe

landing it isn't the problem, but
being responsible for establishing contact
with Echo Base once we land

is the problem. Echo Base!
Those guys don't know from difficulties,

always falling in love with their own lonely voice.
The romantic in me wonders
what there could possibly be to complain about

when I have the capability of watching
one stunning sun after another

burst a million colors in the galactic night.
But it all looks black & white to me,
all those wonders only outlines. Besides,

I have a job to do. The ineffable
something or other? Later for that.

My directives are clear & so what
if there is this thing called the soul
that floats somewhere. I know where I'm going

& I'm focused on that, while all around me
there's such amazing light.

New Year's Eve

It's six o'clock in the evening & where I am
there is no snow. Birds transcribe the incalculable

arc of flight, graceful half-circle etched
between origin & destination. Who can say
where they'll end up? My first name is Nate.

My last name is Pritts. I'm having a wonderful time.
It's been a wonderful year. But even the birds

can't resist taking shots at each other,
thumb-sized beaks aimed kamikaze-style, feathers
shining the gaudy colors of jealousy, avian lust

& rage. My name is Nate & my neighbors
are unknown to me—their names unrecorded,

their haircuts unremarked upon, their all-night-long
comings & goings unexplained, the snap-
crackle-pop of their car tires on the rough gravel

as they back out & pull in with carloads of who-knows-what?
My last name is Pritts. Sluggish winter dark

makes it so I can't see more than ten feet
in front of my face, no moon. My name is Nate
but I will answer to Nathan & after this

last night of the year you can call me The Birdman
for the tenuous but lasting peace I will broker

amongst the warring factions of our feathered friends—
all night we will sing about love & happiness,
our wings our wings our wings around each other.

Breinigsville, PA USA
07 January 2010

230214BV00001B/9/P